Buddhism

This book belongs to

_____

www.pegasusforkids.com

Published by Kuldeep Jain for B. Jain Publishers (P) Ltd., D-157, Sector 63, Noida - 201307, U.P

Printed in India

This graded series is written in easy-to-understand English. The aim is to develop reading habit in children and to increase their vocabulary.

Buddhism is a religion based on the teachings of Buddha, which means 'the enlightened one'.

Buddha is said to have been born as Siddhartha Gautama in the fifth or sixth century BC. Siddhartha was born into a royal family in Kapilavastu.

On his birth, astrologers predicted that Siddhartha would either be a great king or turn his back on power and riches. So, Siddhartha was brought up like a prince, within the walls of the palace by his protective parents.

One day, Siddhartha wanted to step out of the palace and see the world outside.

But Siddhartha didn't know that the king had ordered that the streets be cleared of poor, old and sick people. Siddhartha went out four times and he saw an old man, a sick man, a dead man and a sage.

He realised his world of riches was temporary and sickness, death and poverty could not be avoided.

He also found that the sage was at peace after giving up his life of comfort. Siddhartha was now full of questions. He left behind his life as a prince and his family—parents, wife and son—and went into the forest to seek answers.

In the forest, Siddharta lived a life of a sage and sought answers through years of fasting. This did not help him. He then sat beneath a tree, now called the Bodhi Tree, in Bodhgaya, and vowed not to move until he attained enlightenment.

There, he received enlightenment. Siddhartha then became Buddha and began to teach everyone about life's truths.
His first sermon is said to have been given to five disciples in Sarnath. This event was called the Turning of the Wheel of Law.

Buddha along with his disciples travelled to many places. He spent the next 45 years teaching people 'dharma' (the path to liberation from suffering) and establishing the 'sangha' (a community of monks).

It was after his death that his teachings formed the core foundation of what went on to be called Buddhism.

Three forms of Buddhism are most followed in the world: Hinnayana (Lesser Vehicle), Mahayana (Big Vehicle) and Vajrayana (Diamond Vehicle).
All the three forms are popular in various parts of Southeast Asia.

Buddhism does not believe in a personal God, but the monastic tradition is a key part of Buddhist traditions.

Buddhist monks follow sober and strict practises in all aspects of life. Monks are allowed to accept food, clothing, shelter and medicines. However, strict rules are followed while offering and accepting these things.

Those who follow Buddhism can worship both at home or at a Buddhist temple.

At home, people usually have a small shrine for Buddha where they light candles and incense.

Buddhist temples are spread all over the world. The most popular ones are the pagodas found in China and Japan. Most of these pagados have monasteries near or attached to them.

Besides the pagodas, a typical Buddhist building is the Stupa. Stupas are stone structures built over what are believed to be places where the Buddha gave his sermons.

Buddhist temples are designed to include five elements that they believe to be sacred: Fire, Water, Air, Earth and Wisdom.

Thangka is a form of Buddhist religious art. The subjects include Buddha, bodhisattvas, mandalas etc. Most thangkas are scroll paintings. A key part of worship in Buddhism is the prayer chants, called mantras.

A mantra repeated over and over is believed to bring spiritual peace and awakening.

Another key part of Buddhist worship is prayer wheels and prayer flags. Mantras are decorated on a prayer wheel and the wheel is spun repeatedly. Mantras are also written on a prayer flag.

The most known spiritual master of the Buddhist is the Dalai Lama. The Dalai Lama is the head of the Gelugpa tradition of Tibetan Buddhist. He also won the Nobel Peace Prize in 1989.

A peace-loving religion, Buddhism has many followers throughout the world. It is now one of the major religions of the world.

Buddhism Fact File

- Established 2,500 years ago in India, Buddhism now has over 300 million followers worldwide.

- An important idea in Buddhism is 'karma'. 'Karma' is the belief that past actions, good or bad, will affect, positively or negatively, one's present or future.

- All Buddhist temples carry an image or statue of Buddha. However, the practises of worship depend on which branch of Buddhism one belongs to.

Vocabulary

enlightened	sober
predicted	monasteries
protective	typical
temporary	elements
enlightenment	sacred
liberation	awakening
foundation	spiritual

Activity

Help your child comprehend the story and develop an understanding of values of life through the experiences of the characters. Ask them questions and encourage them to think, ponder and seek answers. This will trigger their critical thinking, creativity and curiosity.

1. When and where was Siddhartha Gautama born?
2. What did Siddhartha do to get answers?
3. What are the three major branches of Buddhism?
4. What is thangka?